# THE TEACHER SAID,

# "MY CHILD CAN'T READ NOW WHAT?"

## CHARMAINE H. DYSON, M.ED.

Sunshine Reigns Publishing (A subsidiary of The Master Communicator's Writing Services)
Houston, Texas
www.mcwritingservices.com

# Testimonials for The Teacher Said, My Child Can't Read ..Now What?

This work is a must have for parents who have struggling readers. The teaching strategies contained therein are backed by 40 years of experience as a highly effective teacher coupled with her passion for teaching as reading as a lifelong skill.  Her techniques are not just based on theory but comes with data and many successes as she witnessed the transformation of struggling readers to fluent readers.
**Liz Allen, Retired Teacher and Assistant Principal**

The author, Charmaine H. Dyson is highly qualified to write this educational guide.  It's full of helpful information for parents, teachers, and students.  Anyone who chooses to use this guide will greatly benefit.  If used as suggested it will ensure what the author intends for it to accomplish.
**Florence M. Jones, Retired Elementary Teacher**

The reading strategies Mrs. Dyson introduced helped my child develop a more calming approach to reading, whereas before reading was thought of as a battle.  With Mrs. Dyson's guidance, she was able to view reading with a new optic.  She told her to think differently that there are words you just have not learned yet, instead of saying, it's too hard to read.
**Bellita Berry, Mother and Grandmother**

# Table of Contents

# Introduction

## The Teacher said, My Child Can't Read... Now What?

You just got a call or email from your child's school stating that he/she is reading below grade level and in danger of failing. All of this was a mystery to you, because every time you see your child, their cell phone is an extra appendage. They have to be able to read to text, read instructions to play video games and use search engines. Something must be wrong with the teacher and the school! You decide to schedule a meeting and when you sit down to talk with the teacher, they show you a reading evaluation that says, "My child can't read!" So now what?

Don't worry. I am here to help! Let's talk about my passion for helping wrestling readers become successful readers. I am going to use the term "wrestling readers" because when watching the children who have difficulty with reading, they wrestle with the words. It looks just like a real wrestling match. (In a wrestling match, the wrestler tries to take control of the opponent by getting behind or on top of him for a "takedown.") It is as if the words on the page are the opponent. When watching a child who is having difficulty reading, you can see and hear them trying to take down the words. They huff and puff, trying to sound the words out. They hope that the word they say will sound right, make sense, and help them know what they are reading. They move around in their seats, rocking back and forth, or cannot sit. They twirl their hair or wiggle their fingers. They crumple the pages of the book or paper, then flip their tablets or technology devices. How do I know? I have taught students for over forty years from Kindergarten to Adults and have seen these behaviors firsthand.

Reading is one of the most essential skills in our society. A child's ability to read and comprehend is key to success in school and life. It is a Daily Life Skill. Reading is a life skill for every occupation. From the brain surgeon to the truck driver, reading is essential. Let's look at a few examples: The cook needs to read the recipe and the orders to fill them correctly. The grocery worker needs to read the boxes to place the correct merchandise on the shelf in the correct area. The mom needs to read the medication to administer to her sick child. The athlete needs to read the playbook. The rapper needs to read the lyrics that he writes. For many children, this task is simple; however, for an ever-increasing number of children, this is quite difficult. It's not just about looking at the pictures and guessing what's on the page. It's not about pronouncing a word softly, so no one hears what was said or skipping a word or even hoping what was said was correct. It's not even about listening to a recording and thinking you know what it is saying. It is really about the letters and sounds, then putting them together; pronouncing the word, and knowing what it means (comprehension). It is really about the alphabet, its sounds, and its connections. Reading starts with words in pictures such as McDonald's, Walmart, Target, Coke, Sprite, and Cheetos. Early readers have a wider vocabulary earlier on in life than non-early readers. This is partly because they are more conscious of the words.

There are 52 letters in the alphabet. Remember singing the alphabet song, thinking there are only 26 letters. These 52 letters of the alphabet (both uppercase and lowercase letters) are noticed when your child begins to have difficulty reading and writing. We haven't even begun to discuss sounds; [initial, medial, final] or even blends, digraphs, and phonemes, but all of these are connected to reading, and the more they are practiced, the more they are mastered.

# Reading encompasses so much:

alphabetic
awareness
(upper/lower case,
letter recognition,
alphabetical sequence,
letter size/shape, phonics
instruction, songs, sound
symbol relation,
onset-rime)

phonological
awareness
(phoneme identification,
phoneme analysis,
phoneme synthesis,
phoneme deletion, phoneme
segmentation, alliteration,
rhymes and poetry, syllable
counting, morpheme
counting)

print
awareness
(title page, the
concept of the title,
author, table of contents,
left to right sweeps; italics,
bold, underline paragraphs,
readings) shared books,
environmental print,
labeling, letter recognition,
punctuation marks

orthographic
awareness
(phonograms,
morphemes, spelling
patterns, word analysis,
word families, letter/sound
mapping, sight words,
decoding skills, inflectional
endings, prefixes-
suffixes, writing
conventions)

reading
comprehension
(guided reading,
connected text story
discussion, fact/opinion,
inference application,
synthesis, outlining, main
idea/details, prediction/
foreshadowing.)

## DON'T BE AFRAID!
## Help is on the way!

What do we do when we believe our child has football, basketball, track, or musical talent? As parents or guardians, we look for opportunities for them to shine.  In most instances, the child begins a program with warm-ups ( better known as drills). This could look like running laps or repeating dance steps or shooting from the free throw line or behind the three-point line.  It is no different for reading. The child needs to know sight words(sometimes called Dolch words, high-frequency words, or Fry words). What do you want your child to excel at? This is the thing that you must focus on. As teachers, we have tons and tons of stories about the students and learning. My grandmother once said, "There is a window to learn certain things and when that window closes, the student may learn, but not at the same rate." It's like starting in a race with everyone else and you begin to run and fall behind.

I am a fourth-generation educator. My great-grandmother, Sarah Moore, and her sister, Carrie Moore Young, were teachers. Carrie was also a supervisor of education in her home area. My grandmother, Ola Banks Fisher, was a teacher and principal for over forty years. She taught elementary, middle, and high school students as well as served as an elementary and high school principal. My mother, Barbara George Hayes, taught Home Economics to high school students and adults while my father, Roy Hayes, taught Vocational Agriculture to high school students and adults.

You must run harder and faster to catch up or remain behind. Many children are very verbal early in life and parents applaud them. They appear smart, however, most of the testing is done visually and not orally. This written testing then shows the student from a different point of view.

Now let's just stop here and say, There's always a miracle or a light bulb coming on. We do not know the time or the place. Many jobs today have training videos, but you must read the subtitles. Some are auditory, but many are visual. Most parents or guardians want their children to be successful. So it is very important to determine if there is some underlying developmental or emotional issue.

# Benefits

I have written this work as a guide to help get you started. You are the parent, guardian, teacher, or other concerned individual that wants to see this child succeed. I believe this guide will greatly benefit parents and children in multiple ways. I don't have all the answers because learning is individual, and it takes hard work and determination.

I want to share seven strategies that may help turn the situation around. These strategies have worked for thousands of children.

## 7 Strategies to Jump Start "Wrestling Reader" Success

This is my perspective from over forty years of teaching, being taught by my parents, teachers, family members, friends, co-workers, classmates, and students, and interviews with parents and teachers. By the way, I'm a fourth-generation educator. You could say that teaching is a family business. My philosophy of education is that "Every Child Can Learn" however the quantity and quality of learning depends on the teacher, the child, and the environment. In my experience, to teach means to show how to guide as well as to impart knowledge.

Use these strategies to create a notebook similar to a playbook so that you and your child can win!

# Don't Panic

You've received the call that your child is having difficulties reading. Maybe it's an exam, diagnostic instrument, or poor grades. Don't Panic! Breathe! Panic is a sudden extreme fear that may cause irrational thoughts or actions. Whatever the case, you begin to internalize that something is wrong or that the teacher is wrong. At this point, the wheels begin to turn and you may be hearing, "Your child is a slow learner and so are you. Oh, you're not a good parent. Your child will not be a success." You might have all sorts of other negative thoughts, but wait, there are other more positive options that you and your child can have.  Here's an empowering method to jumpstart the change called the AAA Method for Wrestling Readers.

### Here's the AAA Method!

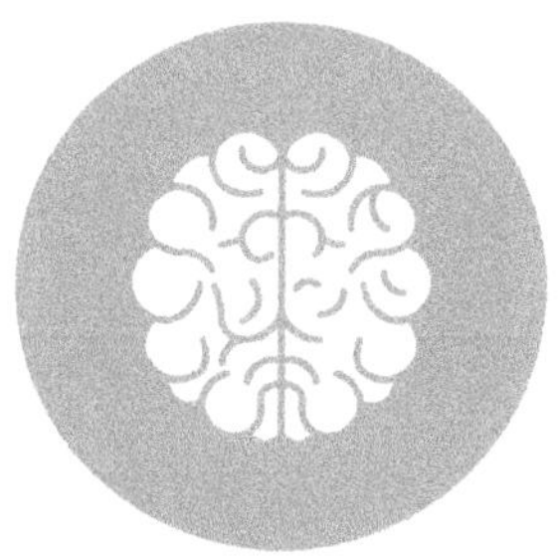

A-Acknowledge
(...there is a problem!)

A-Accept
(...there is a solution!)

A-Achieve
(...a different result, Success!)

By **acknowledging** that there is a problem, gives you the space to begin some change. Acknowledge means to admit the truth. Wipe out all excuses so that you can begin with a clean slate. Be grateful you can make changes and you can. Then give yourself and your child praise. We are on our way.

By **accepting** that there is a solution gives you the space to research more information. Ask more questions of yourself, your child, and the teacher. Accept means that you believe that this information is valid or correct. Recognize that you must **talk to your child and not at them**. There are many programs, materials, resources, and tutors that you can use, but this is a guide to jumpstart you with information and a plan to start and provide maintenance on the road to success. You will need to check in and readjust as your child makes progress.

By **achieving** different results, gives you the space to see a brighter future for all. Achieve means that you and the team(which we will discuss later) will bring about a desired result-SUCCESS! This leads to the second strategic step. It will help you get started.

***Continue to talk to your child through this process rather than at your child's so that you both build confidence in the fact that you are working as a team.

***Continue to talk to your child through this process rather than at your child so that you are working together.

# Get The Facts

What are the facts? A fact is a thing that is known or proven to be true. By facts, I mean data. You have to know where you are starting so that you can document change and celebrate success. You will need to organize a portfolio, such as a three-ring binder. You can always digitize this information and use an electronic resource, such as Google Docs or Microsoft Word. In this section, our goal is to get an accurate snapshot of the child in their present state. That means looking at the whole child, the physical body (state of development), mind (intelligence, brain function, emotional intelligence, academic capabilities), and spirit (the very essence of who they are).

### SECTION 1 - PHYSICAL PROFILE

A.  Recent vision test
B.  Recent hearing test
C.  Recent physical exam

### SECTION 2 - WEEKLY TRACKERS

D.  Weekly Food Tracker - For seven days, write down what your child eats. Make notes if any of the foods made the child sleepy or increased their activity.
E.  Weekly Exercise Tracker - During the seven days, write down what and how much exercise they did.

### SECTION 3 - LEARNING STYLE PROFILE

F.  Latest Reading Levels
G.  Teacher Conference Information
H.  Learning Style Survey
I.  Informal Inventory

### SECTION 4 - DOCUMENTS AND PROGRESS

G.  Report cards
H.  Student Progress
I.  Celebrations

# SECTION 1 – PHYSICAL PROFILE

Child Name ________________________________

Date of Birth ________________________________

Address ________________________________

Parent ________________________________

Vision Test ________________________________

Date ________________________________

Results ________________________________

If glasses are needed, document when they were purchased and when the child begins wearing them.***Special attention is needed to ensure that the child is wearing the glasses. Some students experience peer pressure and would rather not be able to see clearly than experience negative feedback.

Hearing Test ________________________________

Date ________________________________

Results ________________________________

# SECTION 2 - WEEKLY TRACKERS

Directions: Document what your child is eating for two weeks. Use this information to evaluate what foods are influencing your child's learning behaviors. For example: Are they consuming foods that contain a lot of sugar before the school day begins? When are they eating nutritious foods? Are they taking vitamins to supplement nutrients they may be missing in their daily meals?

## WEEKLY FOOD TRACKER

| MONDAY | TUESDAY | WEDNESDAY | THURSDAY | FRIDAY | SATURDAY | SUNDAY |
|---|---|---|---|---|---|---|
| **BREAKFAST** | | | | | | |
| | | | | | | |
| **LUNCH** | | | | | | |
| | | | | | | |
| **DINNER** | | | | | | |
| | | | | | | |
| **SNACKS** | | | | | | |
| | | | | | | |

# WEEKLY EXERCISE TRACKER

Directions: Keep a record of your child's physical activity. For example, they can use their phones to measure how many steps they are taking daily. Encourage them to participate in this activity by making it fun! This will help you determine what physical activities are contributing to their overall well-being and supporting their ability to focus in the classroom.

## WEEKLY EXERCISE TRACKER

| MONDAY | TUESDAY | WEDNESDAY | THURSDAY | FRIDAY | SATURDAY | SUNDAY |
|---|---|---|---|---|---|---|
|  |  |  |  |  |  |  |

# SECTION 3 - LEARNING  STYLE PROFILE

**F.    READING LEVEL** ____________________________________________

**G.  TEACHER CONFERENCE INFORMATION**

Here are some suggested questions that may help you gather facts.

**TEACHER CONFERENCE**

Date            ________________________________________

**1**   Please explain my child's status _________________________________

________________________________________________________________

**2**   What has been done to help my child? _____________________________

________________________________________________________________

**3**   When was this problem discovered? _______________________________

________________________________________________________________

**4**   Who are other specialists/professionals that I can speak to about my child? ______________

________________________________________________________________

**5**   How can I make an appointment with this professional?

Additional Notes ___________________________________________________

________________________________________________________________

**6**   How can I help my child? ________________________________________

________________________________________________________________

**7**   What do you see as my child's strengths? __________________________

________________________________________________________________

## H.  LEARNING STYLE SURVEY

A learning style survey is helpful because it gives a picture of how your child learns. Typically, these learners are divided into several categories, such as visual, auditory, kinesthetic, or read/write. The visual learner thrives when they can view concepts. The auditory learner thrives when they can hear information. The kinesthetic or physical learner thrives and they have hands-on experiences. This survey presents more facts about how your child gathers and processes information. I suggest that you research on Google for a Learning Style Survey that best suits your child's grade level.

A sample can be found at: (https://cf.ltkcdn.net/kids/files/3923-kids-learning-style-survey.pdf)


## I.  INFORMAL INVENTORY

An informal inventory is another way to get facts and information about your child.

Directions: You can make this a game with a reward for its completion. Set aside a special time for you and your child to complete this inventory. Make sure you affirm the successful completion of each statement.

# All About Me

My full name is ___________________________________

My mother's name is ___________________________________

My father's name is ___________________________________

My birthday is ___________________________________

I have ___________________ brothers and ___________________ sisters.

My address  is ___________________________________

___________________________________

My telephone number is ___________________________________

I am ___________________ years old

My favorite food is ___________________________________

My favorite color is ___________________________________

My favorite animal is ___________________________________

My favorite tv show is ___________________________________

# Organize Your Team

Time to organize a team. Organizing means arranging into a structured order. A team is a group ready for some form of competition. In this section, you want to arrange to talk to people who will be on your child's team. They could be family, friends, mentors, professionals, etc. Here's a form to get started. For example, teachers, program coordinators, diagnosticians, speech therapists, administrators, social workers, grandparents, tutors, counselors, youth or children's ministers, coaches, community advocates, or after-school personnel can all be part of your team.

Directions: Have the child identify their team members, and write them on the "My Team" worksheet, then design a Team Tee-Shirt.

# MY TEAM

Team Name   ________________________________

Team Colors   ________________________________

Team Mascot

Team Members

________________________  ________________________

________________________  ________________________

________________________  ________________________

________________________  ________________________

TEAM SHIRT DESIGN

# Gather your Resources

Here's where you gather the support materials that help you succeed in preparing your child to improve their reading capability. Resources are a stock or supply of materials that can be used by a person. You want to start with getting the information from the programs that are being used in your child's school.

**1** Login information from the school software programs that are already in use:

Reading Program _______________________________________________

Username _______________________ Password _____________________

Language Arts  Program _________________________________________

Username _______________________ Password _____________________

Other  Program _________________________________________________

Username _______________________ Password _____________________

**2** Research for free resources.  Here are some options:

- » Storyline Online
- » Rock n Learn
- » K5 Learning
- » Starfall
- » All About Learning Press

**3** Additional resources

Reading Program _______________________________________________

Username _______________________ Password _____________________

Language Arts  Program _________________________________________

Username _______________________ Password _____________________

# Positive Words

Positive simply means good, affirmative, or constructive quality. If your child has a positive attitude about homework, you're more likely to see positive feedback on their report card. Practice giving your child and yourself some positive words, phrases, or cheers. I have listed some starters. Add your own. Be creative. Find what makes you and your child light up.

YOU ARE:

| | | | | |
|---|---|---|---|---|
| Amazing | Awesome | Beautiful | Bold | Brilliant |
| Creative | Daring | Dynamic | Exceptional | Excellent |
| Fantastic | Fearless | Great | Gracious | Happy |
| Incredible | Important | Joyful | Kind | Laser focused |
| Magnificent | Marvelous | Nice | Outstanding | Precious |
| Perfect | Phenomenal | Remarkable | Ready | Special |
| Sensational | Super | Terrific | Tenacious | Top Level |
| Unique | Victorious | Wonderful | Worthy | Zenith |

**Add your own:**

_______________________________________________

_______________________________________________

**SAMPLE PHRASES:**

You're the cherry on top of the sundae! You're the bomb!

You rock! You've got this! You're simply the best!

**Add your own:**

_______________________________________________

_______________________________________________

**CHEERS:**

Hold on, wait a minute, My(Team Name) can win it, win it!

# Do The Work

This is the time for the gut work, the grind: the practice and the drills. In this strategy, you will do the work and document it. It is important to have time set aside for a review. As I said earlier, this is practice time. Make sure you keep a log of the time spent.

Some examples:

1.  Use a timer for reading, such as 15 or 30-minute intervals. This time can be spent reading to an adult. You might want to get the grandparents involved, or a trusted family friend to listen to the student.

2.  Use a recorder app or video on your phone.

3.  Set up a meeting on Zoom, Microsoft Teams, or Google Meets and record the student.

Remember the saying, "Rome was not built in a day."? Give yourself some grace. This situation did not happen overnight, so it will not turn around overnight. It may take six months, a year, or more to see some improvement. But if you keep at it, you will see SUCCESS!

# Celebrate

It's that time! Celebrate the little wins and the big wins. Celebrate the progress. Celebrate perseverance. Mark it down! Commemorate the victory with a special activity!

| Favorite Restaurant | Favorite Food | Favorite Game |
| --- | --- | --- |
| Shopping Trip | New Outfit | New Shoes |
| Movie | Trip | Amusement Park |

Make Your Own List

_______________________________________________

_______________________________________________

_______________________________________________

_______________________________________________

_______________________________________________

_______________________________________________

_______________________________________________

# Summary

This book assists you and your child in making progress and avoiding feelings of despair, fear, or worry. The strategies I have provided have been proven effective through extensive testing over the years. Taking the time to prepare a physical notebook or a digital one will be very beneficial. Although it will require time, effort, and determination, you will ultimately achieve success.

# Tributes

Sarah Moore Wilson (great-grandmother), was a graduate of Mary Holmes Seminary, and a teacher in East Feliciana Parish, Ethel, Louisiana.

Carrie Moore Young (great-great aunt), was a graduate of Tuskegee Institute, and a teacher and supervisor in East Feliciana Parish, Clinton, Louisiana.

Ola B. Fisher (grandmother), was a graduate of Leland College and Tuskegee Institute, and a teacher and principal for over forty years in East Feliciana Parish, Clinton, Louisiana.

Barbara G. Hayes (mother), a graduate of Southern University, and a teacher of Home Economics (high school and adults) for over thirty years in East Feliciana Parish, Clinton, Louisiana.

Roy E. Hayes (father), was a graduate of Southern University, and a teacher of Vocational Agriculture for over thirty years in Bossier Parish, Princeton, Louisiana.

# Acknowledgments

I would like to express my gratitude to my loved ones, close friends, and the countless students I've had the privilege of teaching throughout my extensive four-decade career in the education sector.

# Notes

# Notes

# Notes

# Notes

# Notes